YOU CHOOSE
BOOKS

COULD YOU
ESCAPE
THE TOWER
OF LONDON?

AN INTERACTIVE SURVIVAL ADVENTURE

BY BLAKE HOENA

CAPSTONE PRESS
a capstone imprint

You Choose Books are published by Capstone Press
1710 Roe Crest Drive, North Mankato, Minnesota 56003
www.capstonepub.com

Library of Congress Cataloging-in-Publication Data
Names: Hoena, B. A., author.
Title: Could you escape the Tower of London? : an interactive survival
  adventure / by Blake Hoena.
Description: North Mankato, Minnesota : Capstone Press, [2020] | Series: You
  choose: can you escape? | Summary: Your survival depends on making the
  right choices at key moments when you are eager to escape from the Tower
  of London.
Identifiers: LCCN 2019008533| ISBN 9781543573930 (hardcover) | ISBN
  9781543575637 (paperback) | ISBN 9781543573978 (ebook pdf)
Subjects: LCSH: Plot-your-own stories. | CYAC: Survival—Fiction. |
  Escapes—Fiction. | Tower of London (London, England)—Fiction. | London
  (England)—History—Fiction. | Great Britain—History—Fiction |
  Plot-your-own stories.
Classification: LCC PZ7.H67127 Cs 2020 | DDC [Fic]—dc23
LC record available at https://lccn.loc.gov/2019008533

Editorial Credits
Mari Bolte, editor; Bobbie Nuytten, designer; Eric Gohl, media researcher:
Laura Manthe, premedia specialist

Photo Credits
Alamy: Chronicle, 53, Commission Air, 4, De Luan, 49, Hilary Morgan, 70, London
Images/Paul White, 19, Science History Images, 63, Stuart Robertson, 43, The Picture
Art Collection, 83; Newscom: Heritage Images/City of London: London Metropolitan
Archives, 30, 88, Universal Images Group/Dorling Kindersley, 24; Shutterstock:
Antoine Barthelemy, 58, Arndale, 76, Celso Diniz, 16, Dmitry Naumov, 104, Fedyaeva
Maria, 10, Jeff Whyte, 38, 100, Justin Delano, 6, Keiki, 35, Mistervlad, cover, back
cover, murtaza1112, 68; SuperStock: Interfoto, 97

Printed and bound in the United States of America.
PA70

TABLE OF CONTENTS

TOWER OF LONDON

Map Key:

1. White Tower
2. Bloody Tower
3. Wakefield Tower
4. Byward Tower
5. Traitors' Gate
6. Beauchamp Tower
7. Cradle Tower
8. Tower Wharf
9. Coldharbour Gate
10. Jewel House
11. River Thames

ABOUT YOUR ADVENTURE

YOU are about to step foot into one of the most famous fortresses in the world. In the past, it has served as a home to kings and queens, the United Kingdom's Royal Mint, and even a zoo. It has kept vast collections of weapons, books, and even the Crown Jewels of the United Kingdom. And it has housed prisoners who spent the rest of their lives behind the walls of the Tower.

The choices you make will determine whether or not you become a prisoner yourself. Will you sneak past the prison guards to freedom or be trapped behind the Tower walls forever? You choose the path of your next adventure—or your next failure.

Turn the page to begin your adventure.

Chapter 1

THE FAMOUS PRISON

The Tower of London has a long history, and has served many purposes. First built as a stronghold for early monarchs, the Tower's walls helped them cement their rule over the land.

The central structure, the White Tower, is the oldest building. It stands at nearly 90 feet high and has walls 15 feet thick. It is one of the most famous castle keeps in the world.

An inner and outer wall frame the White Tower. Twenty other towers line the walls. Entrances in the walls and towers, called gates, allow visitors to move about the castle.

A large moat surrounds the outer wall. Throughout history, the moat has been filled with water from the River Thames.

Turn the page.

The Tower of London has served as a seat of power in the United Kingdom and been home to kings and queens. But it is most well known as a prison and place of torture. Starting as early as 1100, spies and traitors were locked up there.

No ruler is without enemies. There is always someone who wants to grab the power of the throne for themselves. But not every attempt can be successful. And after the dust has settled, the nobles who failed need a prison. As a royal castle, the Tower of London is the perfect location.

But traitorous royals and their supporters are not the only inmates. Corrupt government officials and thieves have been held there too. Trying to cheat or rob from the crown is a highly punishable crime.

Those who defy the church can also find themselves behind bars. These prisoners, called heretics, may suffer a horrible experience. They often have to endure painful torture.

The Tower of London is not a place where many would want to be sent. So why are you going? Are you a traitor to the crown? Are you being persecuted for your beliefs? Or are you headed there to visit a friend who is locked up?

If you are a traitor and spy, turn to page page 11.

If you are being persecuted for religious reasons, turn to page page 39.

If you plan to help a friend escape, turn to page page 71.

Chapter 2

A TRAITOR AND SPY

The death of a monarch could throw England into conflict. This was especially true if several people had strong claims to the crown.

In 1376, King Edward III was nearing the end of his life. But Edward's oldest son, known as the Black Prince, had died in June. The prince's son, Richard II, was next in line. He became king the following year when Edward III died.

But Edward III had other sons and grandsons. There were many who could rule England.

In 1399 one of those grandsons made his move. Henry IV forcibly took the throne from Richard II. This set in motion years of fighting between Edward III's descendants.

Turn the page.

Uprisings and rebellions began. Kings ascended to the throne, and kings were deposed.

In 1455, the War of the Roses begins. Henry VI's family, the Lancasters, descended from Edward III's third son, John of Gaunt, and are represented by a red rose. Edward IV's family, the Yorks, are descended from Edward III's fourth son, Edmund of Langley. They are represented by a white rose. The whole country is caught up in the conflict. Many people have to choose who to support and who to fight for—and that includes you.

Both royals are descendants of Edward III. Both have a strong claim to the throne. But who will you choose as your ruler?

If you are a noble supporting Edward IV, go to page 13.
If you are a spy for Henry VI, turn to page 17.

The Lancasters have held the throne for three generations. In 1461 Edward IV used force to take the crown from Henry IV's grandson, Henry VI. You quickly gave your support to the new king.

You were actually one of the few nobles to do so. But you felt that Henry VI was not a fit ruler. He surrounded himself with unpopular, power-hungry nobles, which caused great civil unrest among the people of England.

But now you are paying for that decision. Around ten years later, Henry VI took back the throne. You are labeled a traitor.

One night soldiers take you from your home. They lead you to a dock along the River Thames. You are placed in a boat. It takes you west, toward the Tower of London.

Turn the page.

The night is eerily quiet, except for the splash of the boat's oars in the water. You look up as it passes under the Tower Bridge. In the moonlight, you can just make out a row of spikes sticking up from the bridge. Each spike is topped with the head of someone Henry VI and his supporters accused of being a traitor.

You realize that you could also end up on the chopping block if you are not careful.

Your boat glides up to the Tower Wharf. The castle's outer wall looms ahead. You are taken inside through Traitors' Gate and handed over to a guard.

The guard leads you to a cell in the Beauchamp Tower. This is where you will stay until your fate is decided. This brick-and-stone tower is part of the castle's inner wall.

Because you are a noble, you have certain privileges. Your relatives or servants can send you food and drink. You can walk around the castle grounds under the supervision of your guard. You can also have visitors.

Your stay there should not be horrible. Yet, you are still unsure of your fate. You did oppose Henry VI, the current king. Your name is now tied to the word traitor. And as you saw up on the Tower Bridge, that alone could make you lose your head.

Maybe you could escape. As a noble, you can have your servants bring in anything you might need, including extra food and drink. You could invite the guards to share your treats to celebrate a special occasion. Then, when the guards are having fun, you could sneak out.

Turn the page.

Wealthy prisoners could bring servants and companions. Some royals were even allowed out for shopping trips or to go hunting.

Or maybe you could invite your friends who also supported Edward IV. And if all of your servants bring weapons in under the party food, you could fight your way out together.

To use the party to distract the guards, turn to page 20.

To use the party to arm your friends, turn to page 23.

You have worked for King Henry VI as a spy ever since the War of the Roses began. But despite all of your efforts, Edward IV still manages to take control of the throne in 1461.

This puts you in a dangerous position. You were spying against the person who is now king. You need to flee, or you could suffer persecution.

You make arrangements to leave the country. But before you are able to go, soldiers come to your home. They bind your hands and toss you into the bottom of a boat. You cannot see where you are being taken, but you know instinctively that you are headed for the Tower of London.

You are taken into the castle through the Traitors' Gate. From there, a guard leads you to a cell in the Beauchamp Tower.

Turn the page.

Your stay is not a difficult one, but you are not a favored prisoner. Most of the nobles under guard were also supporters of Henry VI. But the guards seem to pay more attention to them. It's not just because of status, though. It's because of their coin. They have plenty of gold to pay for their needs.

Most days, you are allowed to wander the castle grounds. Your captor is always following you. But following you all day is boring, and he does not pay much attention to what you are doing. If only he realized that what you were doing was thinking of a way to escape.

During your walks, you notice things that have been tossed aside as garbage. You find pieces of metal about the size of your hand. The guards pay you and your scraps no mind as you carry them back to your quarters.

The Tower, and the immediate land around it, covers an area of 18 acres (17.3 hectares).

You can think of two possible uses for them. You might be able to use their rough edges as a file to cut through the bars of your cell. Or you could scrape them against the stone block in your cell to sharpen them for weapons.

To use the pieces of metal as files, turn to page 26.

To use the pieces of metal as weapons, turn to page 29.

There are too many guards roaming the castle grounds for you to have a chance of forcing your way out of the Tower. You need to be sneakier.

The party's on. But instead of inviting friends, you invite as many guards as possible. Before you were imprisoned, you had a reputation as a legendary host. Before, the guards would never have been invited to such an event. Now, they'll be treated like royalty.

Your servants visit as often as they can. Fancy foods and drinks start to crowd your living quarters. It's costing a fortune, but if it helps you escape, it will be worth it.

On the day of the party, the head of your household staff arrives with one last delivery. One of the barrels of wine has a false bottom where a length of rope is coiled. You remove the rope and hide it beneath your clothing.

More than a dozen guards show up to the party. They are more than happy to get away from their posts for a little while. You have a table filled with delicacies waiting for them. You even hired a musician to entertain them.

There is laughing and joking. Stories are told. Music is played. The guards have their fill of food and drink. The noise gets louder and louder.

At the height of the party, you duck outside your cell door. You wait a moment to see if any of the guards follow you out. When none do, you decide that it's time to make your escape.

You exit Beauchamp Tower through doors that lead out onto the ramparts. Beauchamp Tower is part of the inner wall. You'll need to get off this tower and then find a way to escape the outer wall.

Turn the page.

You could tie the rope around one of the tower's battlements and climb down. Then you would need to head toward the Byward Tower Gate, which will lead you over the moat and out of the castle.

Another choice would be to walk along the ramparts all the way to the Traitors' Gate. From there, you could use the rope to lower yourself to the wharf.

To escape through the Byward Tower Gate, turn to page 31.
To escape by heading to the wharf, turn to page 33.

You invite some of your friends to your quarters and tell them your plan. They all think it's a great idea.

You set your plan in motion. You and your friends have servants bring food every day. You tell the guards it is for a party. You also throw in a bribe here or there. After a while, they get used to the servants coming and going with baskets of food. They never check underneath the food. If they did, they would find weapons hidden there.

You are surprised at how easy it is. But then, what makes the Tower of London impenetrable to attacks from the outside also makes it difficult to escape from the inside. Two walls surround the castle grounds. Beyond them is a moat nearly 100 feet wide. Armed guards are stationed at every exit. No one expects you to even try to break out.

Turn the page.

The night of the party comes. About a dozen friends arrive. You invite them in and then shut the door. When you're sure the guards suspect nothing, you open one of the wine barrels. Inside, you find swords and knives. Everyone takes a weapon.

"Are you ready?" you ask. A silent cheer from your allies is the answer you need.

Your personal guard is the first to succumb to your attack. Then you and your friends storm out of the tower. You easily overwhelm the single guard at its entrance.

Beauchamp Tower is shaped like a D. The curved part of the tower faces out.

Next, you head toward the Bloody Tower Gate. This gate will get you out of the castle's inner wall. But as you march across the castle grounds, you hear shouts of alarm. Then you see guards rushing toward you from all directions.

The clang of swords rings through the night air. You try to fight your way toward the exit. You want your freedom so badly. There's no way you can't succeed, you tell yourself. One by one, your friends are cut down around you.

Then you feel the bite of a sword. You scream in pain and collapse to the ground. Your attempt to escape has failed, and you won't be getting a second chance.

THE END

To follow another path, turn to page 9.
To learn more about the Tower of London, turn to page 101.

You think of making weapons out of the metal scraps. But would they really help? The small weapons would not be enough to take out so many guards. Plus, you really have nowhere to hide weapons in your cell.

As they are now, the pieces of metal look like junk. Your captors haven't given them a second glance. Mainly they think you are odd for keeping trash in your cell. But when you test the metal's rough edges on the metal bars of your window, you are happy to discover that they work well as files.

It will take you many days, maybe weeks, to actually cut through the bars. But that gives you time to work on the rest of your plan. You will also need a rope and a grappling hook to make your escape.

Using a rock, you're able to pound the other piece of metal into a hook shape. You only do it at night, using a blanket to muffle the noise. When you're done, you have a workable grappling hook.

During your walks, you pick up any piece of fabric or fiber that you can find. When the time comes for your escape, you will tie or twist them together to make a rope.

When you are finally ready to escape, you need to decide the route to take out of the castle. You could sneak over to the wharf and swim to the other side of the River Thames. But swimming isn't a very common skill. And getting across the River Thames would be difficult, even for an expert swimmer. The river has a strong current, and it is much wider and deeper than the moat.

Turn the page.

You could use the grappling hook and rope to get to the top of the other wall. Then you could climb down into the moat and swim across. The moat is shallower and much less dangerous. But the moat has its drawbacks too. Human waste from the people living at the castle is often dumped into the moat. It will be a smelly stretch of water to swim across.

To swim across the moat, turn to page 35.
To sneak toward the wharf, turn to page 37.

Having a weapon could be your first step to escape. At night, when there are no guards around, you sharpen one end of each of the metal pieces by scraping them against the stone walls of your cell. On the other end of each piece, you wrap strips of cloth to serve as a handle. When done, you have weapons similar to daggers.

One day, your guard takes you away to be questioned. Your captors want to know what information you have about Henry VI. You tell them as little as possible.

When you get back to your cell, you are shocked to see that the head of the guards has searched your belongings. He is holding one of your makeshift weapons.

"What did you plan on doing with this?" he asks, glaring.

Turn the page.

Byward Tower protects the main entrance to the Tower.

You simply shrug your shoulders.

He turns to your guard and says, "Do not let this one wander about anymore."

With that order, your hopes of escaping have been dashed. You are stuck in your cell until your captors decide your fate. Being a spy for a failed king, that could likely be a death by hanging.

THE END

To follow another path, turn to page 9.

To learn more about the Tower of London, turn to page 101.

Any guard leaving the party could come
this way and see you walking on the ramparts.
Climbing down and getting as far away as
possible seems like the best idea. You quickly tie
the rope around one of the battlements and lower
yourself to the ground.

With your feet on solid ground, you stop
for a moment to listen for danger. It sounds like
your party guests are still having a good time.
Everything else is quiet.

You creep along the stone walkway between
the inner and outer walls. You hide in the
shadows until you reach the Byward Tower Gate.
Through this gate is the bridge that crosses the
moat. It is your way out of the castle.

As you had hoped, there are no guards on
duty. They are likely at your party.

Turn the page.

But your feeling of cleverness passes quickly when you discover that the guards locked the gate before leaving their posts. You cannot get it open. You cannot get out of the castle.

You are so close to making your escape. Without thinking, you let out a frustrated cry.

Before you can think of another plan, you hear the sounds of footsteps. Your outburst must have been louder than you realized! There is nowhere for you to go, and the guards soon find you. You are dragged back to your cell and locked inside.

Your plan to escape failed. The next day, you receive horrible news. You have been sentenced to be beheaded as a traitor. You will not have another chance to escape.

THE END

To follow another path, turn to page 9.
To learn more about the Tower of London, turn to page 101.

Your servant had hinted that he might be able to send a boat to wait for you tonight. The wharf seems like it has the most potential for success.

If you drop down from here, you would still have to get through the Byward Tower Gate. There could be guards stationed there. At this time of night, the gate might also be locked.

So you walk along the top of the tower wall toward the wharf. The night is quiet, other than the sounds of laughter coming from your cell.

Your plan to distract the guards is working. No one has noticed that you are gone. The guards who regularly patrol the wall aren't here either. They must be at the party too.

You make your way to Wakefield Tower without being seen. There is a walkway that attaches that tower to the top of Traitors' Gate.

Turn the page.

Once you reach the gate, you tie a rope around one of the battlements and climb down to the wharf.

"Over here," someone whispers.

You look to see friends sitting in a boat. You rush over to them and jump in. They row as fast and as quietly as they can. Every stroke carries you farther away from the prison.

You have escaped the Tower of London!

THE END

To follow another path, turn to page 9.
To learn more about the Tower of London, turn to page 101.

You're not confident enough in your swimming skill to risk the river. You'll just have to bear the filthy moat.

Once you have made a big enough opening in your cell window, you squeeze through. You then crawl over to the top of the inner wall. From there, you use your makeshift grappling hook and rope to lower yourself to the walkway between the inner and outer walls.

Turn the page.

One prisoner escaped the White Tower by climbing out a window and lowering himself to the ground with a rope.

With a yank of the rope, your hook comes loose. You walk over to the outer wall and toss the grappling hook. It catches on the top of the wall. It is a difficult climb. But you eventually reach the top of the other wall.

From there, you hook the rope to one of the battlements. You climb down, carefully lowering yourself into the smelly moat water.

The swim across is not easy. Slick waste coats your clothing. You struggle to breathe because of the stench. But it is a short swim.

After climbing out on the other side, you disappear into the night. You're free!

THE END

To follow another path, turn to page 9.
To learn more about the Tower of London, turn to page 101

The last thing you want to do is swim across the disgusting moat. The Tower Wharf seems like a cleaner, if more dangerous, escape route.

On the night of your escape, you finish cutting through the bars of your window. Then you use your rope to lower yourself to the ground.

Thankfully, there are few people about at night. You see some guards, but they are easy to dodge.

You reach the wharf and dive into the water. At first, swimming is easy. But soon you start to tire. The river's current seems to pull you in every direction. You make it about halfway across when your strength fails you. Your lungs fill with water as you gasp for air. The blackness of the water has you in its grasp. You take your last breath.

THE END

To follow another path, turn to page 9.
To learn more about the Tower of London, turn to page 101.

Chapter 3

RELIGIOUS PERSECUTION

Religion has long played an important part in England's history. Even before the country was united under William the Conqueror, the Roman Catholic Church had made its presence known. The pope and the church's leaders have helped choose England's rulers and have influenced its laws many times.

But the church has become unpopular. Some people think the Roman Catholic Church gives Rome too much power over England. Others feel its leaders have grown rich from corruption. Church leaders collect large sums of taxes, and some of that money ends up in their pockets.

Turn the page.

On top of all that, church services are held in Latin. Most people cannot understand this ancient language. They do not even know what the priests are saying.

Fed up, people broke away from the Roman Catholic Church in the early 1500s. This movement was called the Reformation. A Christian branch of Protestants begins to form. Protestants do not believe the pope holds power over their rulers. They do not follow many of the Roman Catholic traditions. They also hold services in the languages that everyday people speak and understand.

The split from the Roman Catholic Church is not peaceful. Catholic and Protestant church leaders are often in conflict. Wars are fought and riots take place, all because of religious differences.

In England, the current ruler often determines which religion is accepted. Anyone practicing the wrong religion risks being labeled a heretic and is imprisoned.

You are one of those heretics. But who gave you that label, and what did you do? Which ruler will show you mercy—or take your head?

If Edward VI is king, turn to page 42.

If Mary I is queen, turn to page 46.

King Edward VI was crowned ruler of England in 1547. He was just 9 years old at the time. But what is most important is that he was raised Protestant. He is actually the first Protestant ruler of the country.

As a child, King Edward VI does not govern by himself. A regency council of English nobles guides the king's decisions and orders. They are all supporters of the Reformation. Not only does the council believe in breaking from the Roman Catholic Church, they have also created laws condemning many of its practices.

You do not support these rules. You believe people should not be restricted in how they voice their beliefs and opinions. This has put you at odds with those in power. Someone heard your words spoken aloud—and this is why you are being taken to the Tower of London.

Your guard leads you to a cell in the Cradle Tower. He will be the one watching over you while you are locked in the castle. He will bring you your food and see to your needs.

A dock stretches across the castle's now-dry wharf. It stands between the Cradle Tower (far) and the Well Tower (near).

Turn the page.

The tower you are in is part of the castle's outer wall. It faces south, toward the River Thames. The Tower Wharf lies between the outer wall and the river. Boats often dock there to bring prisoners to the castle.

Like most people condemned as heretics, your stay in the Tower is not a pleasant one. You are not given much time to get used to your surroundings before you are taken to be tortured.

A cruel-looking man binds your wrists in metal manacles. Then he has you step onto a wooden stool. The manacles are attached to a hook. The hook has been nailed to a wooden beam high above your head.

Once everything is set, your torturer kicks the stool out from under you. You are left hanging. The manacles dig painfully into your wrists. Your hands swell, and your fingers grow numb.

As you dangle there, your torturer asks you to give up the names of your friends.

"Who are they?" he growls.

If you provide the names of others who share your beliefs, the torture will end, he promises. If not, the pain will continue, and the torture will only get worse. That he also promises.

What do you do?

To end the torture, turn to page 49.
To refuse to speak, turn to page 52.

Queen Mary I was crowned ruler of England in 1553. She came to power shortly after her half brother, King Edward VI, died.

Even though they were siblings, there were big differences in how the two were raised. Edward was a Protestant. Under his rule, England broke away from the Roman Catholic Church.

But Mary is a Catholic. She wants her country to go back to following the church's traditions. She also wants to bring her country back under the pope's authority. She has called for the persecution of those who do not follow Roman Catholic traditions.

You and your friends do not support her. You feel people should be allowed to worship however they want. But you were too loud in your opinion. For this, you are labeled a heretic and are being imprisoned in the Tower of London.

You are locked in a cell in the Cradle Tower. It is part of the castle's outer wall. It faces south, toward the River Thames. A wharf lies between it and the river. Boats often dock there to bring in new prisoners.

Like other heretics imprisoned in the Tower, you are forced to endure severe punishment, including torture.

Your torturer is a bulky man who always scowls when he speaks. One day he lays you down on a device called a rack. Your arms are bound above your head. Your legs are tied down by ropes.

Then your torturer cranks on a wheel at the foot of the rack. It pulls the ropes tight. You feel them bite into your wrists and ankles. Your joints start to ache.

Turn the page.

"Let me know when you are ready to tell us the names of your heretic friends," the torturer says, pausing to give you a moment of rest.

Then he cranks on the wheel again. The ropes pull your arms and legs tight.

He cranks some more.

That is when the real pain begins. The muscles and tendons in your limbs are getting stretched beyond their limits. Your arm and leg bones feel like they are going to pop out of their sockets.

You could end it all if you provide the information that your torturer is asking for. If not, the torture will continue. What do you do?

To keep quiet, turn to page 52.
To end the torture, turn to page 54.

"I will talk," you groan.

The torturer unhooks your manacles, and you crumble to the cold stone floor. Your guard reappears with a chair and a small desk.

You are lifted onto the wooden stool. A well-dressed man who looks like a church leader enters. He sits down at the desk. He places a sheet of paper and writing tools in front of you.

Turn the page.

Stretching a victim's joints could dislocate, or even tear off, a person's limbs.

"I want you to write down the names of all your associates," he says.

You lift your manacled hands. But your fingers will not work right. You cannot hold the pen correctly.

"I can't," you say. "My fingers are numb."

"Then I will make the list for you," the man grunts.

He picks up the pen and starts writing down the names that you tell him.

When you are done, your guard removes the manacles. He helps you back to your cell, where you collapse on a bed of straw.

You are not put through any more torture. You are thankful for that. But you have just condemned people you know to a cruel fate.

Days later, you are released from the Tower. When you return home, you learn that all your friends and allies have either been captured or have fled the country. Some will suffer as you did. Others will be on the run for the rest of their lives. What you have done leads to many restless nights of sleep for you.

THE END

To follow another path, turn to page 9.
To learn more about the Tower of London, turn to page 101.

"I will tell you nothing," you growl.

You know that giving up the names of your friends will condemn them to this same fate. Some may be executed.

So you keep quiet. You endure the pain. At one point, you pass out.

Your torturer leaves you in a crumbled heap on the cold stone floor. Your guard manages to get you back to your cell.

You cannot fall asleep. Your whole body aches. Groans of agony seem to be the only sounds you can make.

You know that you cannot survive much more of this treatment. You need to escape. Maybe if you can contact your friends, you can find a way out of the Tower.

Lady Jane Grey was queen for nine days. She ruled after Edward VI and before Mary I. She was executed at the Tower on February 12, 1554.

But for that to happen, you will need help. The only two people you see consistently are your torturer and your guard. You have no other choice than to ask if one of them will aid you in getting a message to your friends. It seems like a crazy idea, but what else can you do?

Whose help do you seek?

To ask for help from your torturer, turn to page 56.

To ask for help from your guard, turn to page 58.

You hear a popping noise. Then your body burns with pain. "Stop! Stop!" you yell. "I will tell you all I know."

The torturer unties your wrists and ankles.

He and your guard fetch two chairs. They help you into one of the chairs. You have difficulty sitting upright, and they have to tie you to yours.

Moments later, another man enters the room. He is dressed in the robes of a church leader.

"I hear you are ready to speak," he says, sitting in the other chair.

You nod. You answer all of his questions, no matter how personal. You give him the names of your associates. You also confess to beliefs that oppose the Roman Catholic Church.

When you are done, you wait for relief. You expect to be taken back to your quarters and cared for. You do not expect what comes next.

"There will be no more torture," your confessor says. "But since you admit guilt, you will be burned at the stake as a heretic." He leaves without seeming to hear your cries.

You are taken back to your cell and put in chains. There, you stay until the day of your execution.

THE END

To follow another path, turn to page 9.
To learn more about the Tower of London, turn to page 101.

Your torturer sees how you are suffering. He knows the pain you are in and hears your cries of agony. Perhaps this will make him sympathetic to you.

One day as he is binding your wrists, you whisper, "You don't need to do this."

He says nothing. He continues his work without making eye contact.

"I have friends," you say. "Friends with money. A *lot* of money."

This gets his attention. He turns and stares you in the face.

"You think maybe you can bribe me?" he asks. "Then I'll be gentle with you?"

"No, no, I want you to help me escape," you whisper. "My friends will pay you generously."

He scoffs at that and binds your wrists extra tight. You wince in pain.

"If I did that," he says, "I'd end up right where you are now."

He does not show you any mercy.

You scream in agony.

Eventually the pain will be too much for you. Either you will die at the hands of your torturer or you will give up the names of your associates. No matter which happens, you are in for many long days of suffering.

THE END

To follow another path, turn to page 9.
To learn more about the Tower of London, turn to page 101.

You doubt your torturer would help you. After all, he is the one causing you all the pain. That is his job, and he is a professional.

But your guard might be kinder. It is actually common for guards to do favors for inmates. And it is his job to watch over you. He is the one who helps you back to your cell after you are tortured.

Prisoners were kept at the Tower between 1100 and 1941.

One night you ask him, "Could you take a message to my friends? I will pay you."

"I will," he agrees, nodding. "Just tell me what you need."

You will need paper and writing tools to send messages. But if you are going to hatch an escape plan, you do not want your guard reading what you write. Perhaps you could write secret messages, like a spy. You know the juice of an orange will produce clear ink. When heated, the letters will appear.

You could ask for a candle instead. You could use drops of heated wax to seal to your letters. If the letters arrived with their seals broken, your friends would know they had been read.

To ask for a candle, turn to page 60.
To ask for oranges, turn to page 62.

"Could you bring me some writing supplies?" you ask. "And a candle?"

"As long as you have the money to pay for it, I can get whatever you need," he says.

"That won't be a problem," you say, winking. Prisoners are allowed to have money to pay for the things they might need. You came in with plenty.

Once you have your supplies, you write a note to a trusted ally. In it, you mention ideas for an escape. Then you seal the letter with wax. You give the letter to your guard. You trust him not to break the seal.

The next day your guard enters your room. His superior follows behind. While your guard looks down at his feet, ashamed, the other man rummages through all of your things. He takes your writing supplies, any food you have, and all your money.

Then he turns to you. "Let's see you escape now!" he says triumphantly.

As he walks out of your cell, he turns to your guard. "I want this prisoner locked in chains at all times," he says.

"He saw the letter," your guard explains. "I had no choice but to let him read it."

He binds your wrists and ankles in heavy chains. You can hardly walk. And you are denied any contact with the outside. Now you have no hope of escape. You prepare to spend many days in the Tower enduring agonizing torture.

THE END

To follow another path, turn to page 9.
To learn more about the Tower of London, turn to page 101.

"I could use some writing supplies," you say, "and also a sack of oranges."

Your guard does not think twice about this request. As long as you have money, he can get anything you need—within reason.

You write a note with regular ink on one side of the paper. You ask for books to read and for news about your family. You leave small sketches around the edges of the paper. One of the sketches is of a candle. Hopefully your friends will understand what to do.

Once you have the oranges, you break one open. You eat half. Then you dip a sliver of wood into the other half. You use the wood like a pen to write a message with the fruit juice on the other side of the paper. In your secret message, you ask for an item to help you escape.

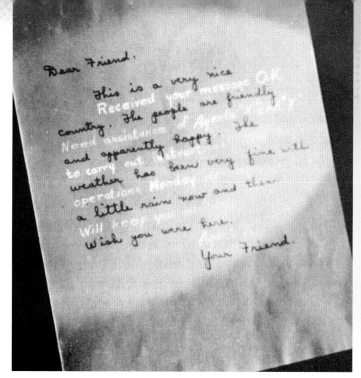

Spies have made invisible ink out of simple things such as orange or lemon juice, oatmeal and milk, and urine.

But what item will help you the most? You could use a weapon. With a dagger, you might be able to fight your way out of the castle. Or you could ask for a rope. You could use it to lower yourself down the outer wall of the castle.

To sneak in a rope, turn to page 64.
To sneak in a weapon, turn to page 67.

You doubt a weapon would really help you much. You would have to fight your way past your guard as well as any others patrolling the castle. They are all armed with pikes, which are sharp blades attached to long poles. You'd never get close enough to land an attack. You would do better to sneak away.

In your secret note, you ask for a rope. It arrives inside a hollowed-out loaf of bread, along with a message. Your friends will meet you in a boat at the Tower Wharf. You will just need to find a way to get there on the chosen night.

"It's so nice out," you say to the guard on the night of your escape. "Do you mind if I go for a walk along the walls?"

You slip him some coins. He nods and lets you go off alone.

The wall you walk along is known as a rampart. It is wide enough to have a stone walkway down the middle. Rectangle-shaped battlements line the outer edge facing the wharf.

When you peek through the battlements, you can see the shadow of a small boat heading toward the wharf. It is time for you to escape.

You have been carrying the rope under your shirt. Now you tie it around a battlement. Then you toss the other end over the edge of the wall. It's time to climb.

But when you reach the end of the rope, you are still dangling in the air. It's dark and you can't tell how far you are from the ground. But down is the only way you can go. Even if you had the strength to pull yourself back up, you would be climbing back to prison and torture.

Turn the page.

You let go. You drop for what seems like forever. Sharp pain shoots up your leg when you hit the ground. But it must not have been a far drop. Other than shock and some immediate pain, you're OK.

"Hurry, guards are coming," you hear someone whisper.

You hobble over to the boat as fast as you can. Your friends tell you to lie down. They cover you with a heavy tarp.

The boat slips away in the night. You are on your way to freedom.

THE END

To follow another path, turn to page 9.
To learn more about the Tower of London, turn to page 101.

You decide a weapon will serve you best. Your friends must have understood your note, because one day you find a dagger tucked into some clothing they have sent.

After a few more secret notes, you arrange for your friends to meet you at the Tower Wharf. Now it's up to you to get there.

On the night of your planned escape, you wait for your guard to bring you dinner. With dagger in hand, you force him to give you his keys. Then you lock him in your cell.

"Stay quiet," you whisper. "I'll see to it you're rewarded for it." He scowls, but nods.

You head down several flights of stairs and exit the tower. Unfortunately the door to the tower is on the inside of the castle. The Tower Wharf, where your friends will meet you, is outside.

Turn the page.

You need to find a door on the outer wall. You look at your guard's keys, but you can't tell which key is for what door.

But you've made a mistake. You have stood in the open for too long. A guard has spotted you.

a view of the River Thames, looking toward the White Tower and the Tower Wharf

"You there, stop!" he shouts.

You try running away from him. But before you get too far, you are met by another guard. With dagger in hand, you attack. He meets your charge with his pike, a long wooden shaft tipped with a steel blade. Trained to watch over the royal prison, the guard is an expert with his weapon. Its long shaft ensures the guard never comes close enough for you to attack. Even if you could get to him, you are only fair at hand-to-hand combat. It's no match. The guard buries the pike's steel tip in your gut. You fall to the ground, the dagger sliding out of your grasp. Death is your escape from the Tower of London.

THE END

To follow another path, turn to page 9.
To learn more about the Tower of London, turn to page 101.

Chapter 4

HELPING A FRIEND ESCAPE

It is a scary time in England. People you once thought of as friends have turned on one another. One remark made at the wrong time can be dangerous—or even deadly.

You are about to see the consequences of trusting the untrustworthy today. In your pocket you carry a note from a good friend. It reads:

I have been accused of a crime and imprisoned in the Tower of London. Please visit, if you can.

You are worried about your friend, so you decide to go. You know that the Tower has a bad reputation. Prisoners there have been brutally tortured, and worse. Some are even publicly executed for their crimes.

Turn the page.

Luckily your friend has not committed any religious crimes. Usually it is heretics who receive the worst treatment. They are often tortured.

Traitors and thieves are treated less harshly. If they are wealthy, they may even hold parties while imprisoned.

Your friend isn't lucky enough to be a noble. But, like most prisoners, your friend is free to have visitors.

If you are visiting your friend William, go to page 73.
If you are visiting your friend Alice, turn to page 78.

When a queen or king dies without an heir, sometimes Parliament chooses the next monarch. That is how George Louis became King George I after the death of his cousin, Queen Anne.

But some thought James Francis Edward Stuart had a better claim to the throne. After all, he was Queen Anne's younger brother.

Your friend William was among those who supported James. He had joined a failed rebellion against the king. For that, William was charged with treason and taken to the Tower of London.

You cross the moat surrounding the castle. You enter the outer wall through the Byward Tower Gate. Then you walk along a stone pathway until you reach the Bloody Tower Gate, which is an entryway into the castle's inner wall.

Turn the page.

William is being held in the Bloody Tower. Once known as the Garden Tower, this building has earned a dark reputation. You climb several flights of stairs to get to your friend's cell.

"How are you, Will?" you ask upon entering his room.

He is sitting at a desk and reading a book. He looks tired, with dark circles under his eyes. You wonder how much weight he has lost in just the short time he has been here.

"OK," he says with a weak smile. Then he looks down at his feet.

"What's wrong?" you ask. "They aren't torturing you, are they?"

"No, no, not for my crimes," he says. "It's just that . . ." He looks up to meet your eyes. "For supporting the rebellion, I'm to be executed."

"When?" you ask, shocked.

"In a matter of days," William replies.

You can't believe what you are hearing.

"I will get you out of here," you whisper to your friend. You have no idea how you will do it. But you promise yourself—and him—that you will.

As your visit continues, he begins to sound more and more hopeful. You think of the way he looked when you first arrived. You think of how heartbroken his family would be if he was gone. There is no way you can fail him. But how will you free him?

On your way out of the castle, you carefully observe the people around you. You hope they might give you some inspiration.

Turn the page.

You notice the yeomen warders in their bright red uniforms. King Henry VII formed this order of the guard at the Tower after he won the War of the Roses in 1485. They are posted at each gate. Others patrol the hallways. They seem to freely go about their business.

Yeoman warders are part of the royal guard. They are also known as beefeaters.

There are also many people wandering around. You guess that some of them live on the castle grounds. But others, like you, must be here to see friends and family who have been imprisoned.

You watch as one couple walks through a tower gate. A yeomen stops the man and checks the package that he carries. The guard does not even question the woman.

An idea is forming. You can have your friend disguise himself. He could put on a yeomen's uniform and simply walk right out of the castle. Or he could dress up as a woman, and you could escort him out.

To disguise your friend as a yeoman, turn to page 81.
To disguise your friend as a woman, turn to page 85.

You are shocked to learn that your friend Alice was jailed for piracy. Usually pirates are sent to regular prison, not the Tower of London. She is also being kept in the Coldharbour Gate, a fort within the inner walls of the castle.

To get to Alice, you had to cross a moat. Then you passed through the outer Byward Tower Gate. After that, you went through the Bloody Tower Gate and into the heart of the fortress.

You stare up at the building. Two cylinder-shaped towers join together to make Coldharbour. They share an edge with the White Tower. Paths edged with battlement walls join the cylinders to the Bloody Tower. This is one of the best-protected places in the entire Tower of London.

"I didn't do it!" Alice says the moment you step into her cell.

You sigh. "Then what *did* happen?" you ask.

"It was the captain of the ship I was aboard," she says. "He stole a chest of gold that belonged to the king and laid the blame on me."

Alice is your friend. She is not a thief, and she definitely is not foolish enough to steal from the king. That is a crime that could lead to harsh punishment.

"Did they say how long you are to be held here?" you ask.

"Until the king gets his gold back," she answers, frowning. "At least, that is what I've been told."

It could be a long time until they find the treasure—if they ever find it. You feel that your friend has been falsely accused of a crime. You want to get her out of here. That means helping her escape, if you can.

Turn the page.

"I will find a way to get you out," you say gallantly.

"But how?" she asks.

You peek out the cell's tiny window. It would be easy enough for her to squeeze out. All she would need is a rope. She could use it to lower herself down to the ground.

You examine the rest of the cell. You notice something odd about the door. There is a wide gap underneath, and the bolt holding the single hinge is loose. Someone could pry it open with the right tool.

What do you smuggle into the Tower to help Alice escape?

To smuggle in a rope, turn to page 87.
To smuggle in a stick, turn to page 90.

If you dress William as a guard, he'll also be armed. The thought of a backup weapon gives you a sense of confidence and security.

First, you need a yeoman's uniform. You bribe a local tailor to make one for you. He makes some of the clothes for the nobles in the Tower and knows what the uniforms look like in detail. You pay well, and he works fast.

Next, you need to sneak the uniform into William's cell. For that, you ask for help from another friend, Betty. Each of you hides part of the disguise under your normal clothes. Betty also carries the boots in a bag she covers with a blanket.

All goes well when you enter the castle. Guards nod to you as you walk through the gates. No one checks the bag that Betty carries.

Turn the page.

You head up the flights of stairs to William's room. He quickly changes while Betty stands guard.

Everything is set. Now you just need to make it out of the castle.

You and Betty will leave first. Then William will follow. If all goes as planned, you will meet on the other side of the moat.

You walk down the stairway and then linger at the bottom. William is not far behind. People step aside for him out of respect.

You hold your breath as you walk through the Bloody Tower, but nobody stops you. Now just through the Byward Tower Gate, and William will be free.

But about halfway to the outer gate, someone calls out. "You there. What are you doing here?"

The Bloody Tower entrace allows visitors to pass through the inner wall.

You glance behind to see a couple of the guards blocking William's path.

"I don't recognize you," one guard says.

"I'm new," William tries to explain.

Turn the page.

The first guard shakes his head. Then he takes a closer look at William's face. "You look like that prisoner up in the Bloody Tower."

William panics. As the guards begin to grapple with him, you and Betty turn and walk calmly away. You cannot help him. You cannot afford to be captured. You have no other choice.

That night, you receive news from William. His execution has been moved to the next day. Time is up. You have lost your opportunity to save your friend.

THE END

To follow another path, turn to page 9.
To learn more about the Tower of London, turn to page 101

The yeomen all live at the castle. You are afraid that they will notice a new face in uniform. They might even recognize him as a prisoner. The way the guards ignored the women at the fortress makes you confident that disguising William as a woman is the best choice.

For William's disguise, you get help from another friend, Betty. She agrees to wear two dresses and carry a wig and makeup with her into the castle.

The next day, you both go to see William. You pass by guards at each gate. Not one of them checks the bag that Betty carries. They are used to seeing you come and go.

Inside his cell, William changes into the spare dress. You and Betty help him with the wig and makeup.

Turn the page.

You take a step back. While it is not a perfect disguise, it will do—as long as no one stops William and looks too closely.

"Now what?" he asks.

The guards saw you and Betty enter the tower together. Although you don't feel as though they paid you a lot of attention, they might have. They will be expecting two people to walk out together. Three people leaving together at the same time would be too obvious.

You could send William out first, by himself. Then you and Betty could follow. But would it be safer for Betty and William to leave as a pair?

To send William and Betty together, turn to page 92.
To make William go alone, turn to page 94.

If you bring Alice a rope, she can escape on her own. You hide the rope in a package of clothing. It is actually not uncommon for people to bring things to people staying in the prison. You have no doubts that this idea will work.

But as you pass through one of the castle's gates, a yeoman stops you.

"What do you have there?" he asks.

"Just some clothes for a friend," you say.

"Let's have a look then," he says.

"Are you sure?" you ask. You fumble, trying to find a coin to slip him.

"Are you trying to bribe me?" the guard roars. His face turns as red as his uniform. "I'm one of the king's royal bodyguard, and you think I can be bribed? With that?"

Turn the page.

Other guards have appeared. They hold you and search your things. They find the rope right away. Then you are taken to the White Tower.

"You think it's easy to escape the Tower?" the guard asks. "Let's see you get out of Little Ease."

Little Ease is in part of the dungeon under the White Tower. It is only 4 feet (1.2 meters) square and has no windows.

"No," you beg. "Not there!" You have heard the stories. Little Ease is the most famous torture cell. It is only a few feet wide and a few feet tall. It is not tall enough for you to stand in, and it's not long enough for you to lie down.

When you see the heavy wooden door, you struggle to get free. But there is no escape. The guard shoves you inside and the door slams shut behind you.

You are in darkness for what could be eternity. The time spent in Little Ease is horrible. You are cold and sore from lying curled up in a ball on the stone floor. You have no idea when you will get out—if ever.

THE END

To follow another path, turn to page 9.
To learn more about the Tower of London, turn to page 101.

It would be easy enough for Alice to squeeze out of a window and crawl out of her cell. But then what? Someone would likely see her scaling down the side of a tower. Instead, you will bring her a stick. You hope she can use it to pry open her cell door.

When a yeoman sees it tucked in with the other things you are bringing Alice, he gives you an odd look.

"She likes to whittle," you lie.

The guard shrugs but lets you by. What he does not notice is that the clothes you carry are actually from your own closet.

The plan is for Alice to work on the loose hinge with the stick. She should be able to get the door open enough to slip out unnoticed. Then she will leave, dressed in some of your clothes.

The guards have seen you visiting her often. You are both small and slim, and your hair is a similar length and color. You hope that they will assume she is you.

You also make a point to say hello to the guards every time you visit. You want them to be used to seeing you coming and going. You also always wear the same outfit, which is similar to the clothes you brought Alice.

On the day of her escape, you need to decide where you'll be. Will you wait outside the castle for Alice and let her sneak out herself? Or should you visit one last time to help with her escape?

To wait, turn to page 96.

To go see her, turn to page 98.

"You two go ahead," you say. "I will stay."

You watch as your friends leave. They walk arm in arm down the hallway. When a guard approaches, William looks down and whispers something in Betty's ear. The guard walks past without blinking.

Meanwhile, in William's cell, you pretend to have a conversation with William.

"It looks like nice weather we are having," you say, trying to sound like your friend.

"Yes, it is a lovely day," you say in your voice.

"Do you have any news of my family?" your "friend" asks.

You continue on like this with hope that the guards will not get suspicious. You want them to think that William is still in his cell.

When you tire of talking to yourself, you leave the cell. By now, your friends should be well clear of the main gate. You quietly slip out and close the door behind you.

"I wouldn't bother the prisoner," you say to the guard on duty. "He's sleeping."

The guard simply nods as he walks by.

You see Will again at your house. While he has escaped the Tower of London, you know that he is far from safe. He will have to flee England. But living far from home will be better than having to face the executioner.

THE END

To follow another path, turn to page 9.
To learn more about the Tower of London, turn to page 101.

The guards saw you and Betty enter the Bloody Tower together. It might be odd if you do not leave together too.

So you have William leave first. You and Betty count to 100 and then follow.

As you approach the exit to the tower, you can see a small crowd forming. You are horrified to see that the yeoman guarding the tower has grabbed William.

"Well, what have we here?" the guard asks, smirking and poking William.

William says nothing.

"I don't recall you entering the tower," another yeoman says.

"Looks kind of like one of our prisoners," the first says. "Only in a bad disguise." He grabs the wig from William's head. The crowd cheers.

You and Betty try to hurry through the gate before anyone notices. But you're not fast enough. A yeoman spots you.

"You there!" he shouts. "You were visiting this prisoner!"

You do not know what else to do but to turn and run. Betty follows. But the crowd has grown too large and there is nowhere to go. You are quicky cornered and caught.

You and Betty are thrown into a cell. You are not allowed to leave until after William's execution.

THE END

To follow another path, turn to page 9.
To learn more about the Tower of London, turn to page 101.

You decide to meet Alice at your house. You worry that if you go to the prison today, the guards might notice two people dressed alike.

Instead, you prepare for Alice to leave the country once she escapes. The authorities will be looking for her. It won't be safe for her to stay in the area. You pack some of her things and arrange passage aboard a ship headed to France.

Then you wait.

And wait.

The sun sinks below the horizon, and there is still no sign of your friend. You begin to worry.

But then you hear a soft rap on your door. You peek outside, and there she is.

"Quick, get inside," you say.

The conflict between Roman Catholics and Protestants was known as the English Civil War (1642–1651).

"Sorry it took me so long," she says. "I wanted to make sure nobody tried to stop and talk to me. I had to take a roundabout way to get here."

None of that matters now. Alice is safe!

THE END

To follow another path, turn to page 9.
To learn more about the Tower of London, turn to page 101.

You decide to go to the prison one last time. You want to make sure Alice has everything she needs to escape. And you can't just sit at home waiting and wondering.

Like every other visit, you nod to the yeomen guarding Coldharbour. This time, though, he stops you. "Weren't you here earlier?" he asks.

"N-no," you stammer.

"Are you sure?" he asks, squinting. "I swear I saw someone . . ." He frowns. "I better take you up."

Nervous, you follow him up the stairs. You don't like this. He knows you know where to go. You don't need a guide.

When you reach the cell, you can see that the door has been pried open. You arrived too late. Alice has already escaped.

The guard turns to you. "You helped her, didn't you? I knew I saw someone dressed like this before."

You yell and scream, but they ignore you. You are shoved into the cell that was once Alice's.

"We are keeping you here until we find her," a guard says. "Then we'll decide what to do."

Another guard secures the door. He breaks the stick in two before tossing it out the window. Then he tightens the door's loose hinges.

If the guards find Alice, she will surely be punished. If they do not catch her, you have no idea when you will be let out of the cell.

All you can do is wait and hope your punishment is not too severe.

THE END

To follow another path, turn to page 9.
To learn more about the Tower of London, turn to page 101.

Chapter 5

THE TOWER OF LONDON

In 1066 William the Conqueror defeated several powerful English lords at the Battle of Hastings. With this victory, he sealed his claim to the English throne. William then went on to unite all of England under his rule. He served as king of England until his death in 1087.

William had the Tower built on the outskirts of London, near the banks of the River Thames. The Tower provided a place for William to rule from. It also protected the city from attack.

As new rulers came into power, the castle grew. A ring of smaller towers was built around the White Tower. These smaller towers were connected by walls to encircle the castle grounds. An outer wall was eventually added.

A moat was dug and filled with water from the River Thames. Other buildings were constructed, such as a chapel and a barracks for soldiers. Over time, the single tower that William had built became a fortress. Today, all of its buildings and towers are collectively known as the Tower of London.

Among the Tower's many uses, it is best known for being a prison and a place of cruel torture. Its history of famous inmates and executions has also earned the Tower of London the reputation of being one of the most haunted places in the world. Many people believe that the spirits of people who were killed there roam the grounds. There are even stories of a ghostly bear, believed to have once been part of the Royal Menagerie.

Over the course of its history, thousands of people have been imprisoned in the castle. Prisoners range from traitors to the crown to spies, assassins, corrupt government officials, religious heretics, and deposed kings and queens. Most were eventually released. Hundreds were executed for their crimes. And nearly 40 people actually escaped.

The first to do so was Ranulf Flambard in 1100. He simply held a party for some of the guards and then snuck out while they were distracted. Others used disguises. Some escapees had ropes smuggled in and climbed down the castle's walls. Prisoners have swum across the moat or had boats pick them up at the Tower Wharf. One inmate actually used orange juice as invisible ink to send secret messages to friends to arrange an escape.

The Tower of London did not have the security measures that modern prisons have. As a result, many escape stories sound surprisingly simple and even somewhat unbelievable. But when they were taking place, prisoners were treated very differently. Most were allowed to roam the castle grounds with only a guard watching over them. Some even bribed their guards to let them wander around by themselves.

The White Tower has four stories. The entrance is on the first story, not the ground floor.

Wealthy people could have food and clothes brought in to them. This gave them a chance to have items like ropes and weapons smuggled in with other supplies.

Today, the Tower of London serves other purposes. It is no longer used as the country's seat of power or as a prison. Now it is mostly a museum and a tourist attraction. Stories of the ghosts lurking about its grounds and the many strange escape attempts attract visitors from all over the world. Some also come to see the Crown Jewels, which are locked away in the Jewel House. It is an incredible place to visit and study.

TIMELINE

CHAPTER 2: A TRAITOR AND SPY

June 1377: Edward III dies

1377: Richard II rules

1399: Henry IV rules

1413: Henry V rules

1422: Henry VI rules

1455: The War of the Roses starts when Richard, Duke of York, leads the Yorks at the First Battle of St. Albans

1461: Edward IV rules; he is the first York king

1470: Henry VI takes the crown back

1471: Edward IV takes the crown back

1483: Edward V rules from April 9 to June 25

1483: Richard III rules; he is the last York king

1485: Henry Tudor defeats Richard III at the Battle of Bosworth Field; this ends the War of the Roses; Henry marries Edward IV's daughter, Elizabeth, and crowns himself Henry VII

CHAPTER 3: RELIGIOUS PERSECUTION

1547: Edward VI rules

1553: Mary I rules

1558: Mary I dies; Elizabeth I is crowned

CHAPTER 4: HELPING A FRIEND ESCAPE

1714: George Louis is crowned; he rules until 1727

REAL ESCAPE ATTEMPTS

1100: Ranulf Flambard became the Tower of London's first official prisoner. He was also its first escapee. Flambard was jailed for being a corrupt government official. Because he was wealthy, he could afford to have food and wine brought to him while imprisoned. In a barrel of oysters, he had a rope smuggled into the Tower. One night, he invited the guards into his cell for a celebration. While the guards were busy, Flambard slipped away. He squeezed through a window and used the rope to lower himself to the ground.

1413: Sir John Oldcastle was labeled a heretic by his enemies. His religious views differed from those of the Catholic Church. This led to his imprisonment in the Tower of London.

But Oldcastle was popular amongst his supporters. They liked that he voiced his opinions and stood up for those who shared his beliefs. Instead of sneaking him out, his friends snuck into the castle and broke him out. Time and time again, Oldcastle narrowly escaped recapture. But his luck ran out in 1417, when he was finally caught and sent back to the Tower. Shortly afterward, he was hanged over a burning pyre.

1597: John Gerard was a Catholic priest who was persecuted after Protestants came into power. He was captured in 1594 and sent to the Tower in April 1587. Kept in the Salt Tower, he was repeatedly tortured, but never gave up any information.

With the warder's help, Gerard was able to obtain writing materials to send messages to his friends. But he did not just ask for pen and ink. He also asked for a sack of oranges. Using orange juice, he was able to hide secret messages on the letters. The messages, written in juice, could only be seen if the paper was heated. Gerard was able to arrange for a prison break through these secret messages.

One night in 1597, he and another prisoner, John Arden, made their escape. Arden had been kept in the Salt Tower, which was next to the Cradle Tower. The men became friends. They convinced guards to let them meet to pray.

Gerard asked his friends to bring a rope to the Tower. One end of the rope would be staked across the moat. They brought the other end of the rope to the wall. Gerard let down a length of heavy thread, which his friends tied to the rope. Gerard was then able to pull the rope to the top of the tower.

Gerard and Arden slid down the rope and across the moat and to the wharf. There, Gerard's friends were waiting with a boat as a getaway vehicle.

Gerard took care to protect his warder from punishment. He arranged for the warder's passage to a safe house and gave him money to replace his lost wages.

Although free, Gerard eventually had to leave the country. He slipped out disguised as a servant to the Spanish ambassador.

1716: The Earl of Nithsdale was sent to the Tower of London for treason. He had supported one of the king's rivals. Days before he was to be executed, his wife and her maid came to visit. Under their clothes, they snuck in a disguise for the earl. He dressed up as a woman. His wife even brought him a wig and white makeup to cover up his beard.

The Earl and the maid walked out of the castle. His wife stayed behind in his cell. She pretended to talk to her husband so that the guards would not get suspicious about the escape attempt. They did not realize that the earl had left his cell until he was safely away.

OTHER PATHS TO EXPLORE

◆ Prisoners at the Tower of London had a surprising amount of freedom. Some were able to bribe their warders into letting them visit other inmates. How might being able to talk to another prisoner aid in your escape plans?

◆ The Tower of London is thought to be one of the most haunted places in the world. Many people have died there cruelly, from Queen Anne Boleyn, the second wife to King Henry VIII, to Lady Jane Grey. She was queen for just nine days before Mary I took the crown from her and had her executed. The ghosts of both Anne Boleyn and Jane Grey are said to haunt the castle. How might one of the many ghosts lurking about the Tower of London help in planning an escape?

◆ One means of planning an escape was by sending secret messages to friends. One escapee actually used orange juice like an invisible ink to send such messages. But there are many other ways, from messenger pigeons to secrets codes that can be used to send messages. What other methods could be used to send messages as well as get items into (or out of) the castle?

READ MORE

Boutland, Craig. *Ghoulish Ghosts*. Minneapolis: Lerner Publications, 2019.

Hoena, Blake. *Tower of London: A Chilling Interactive Adventure*. North Mankato, MN: Capstone Press, 2017.

Pascal, Janet B. *Where is the Tower of London?* New York: Penguin Workshop, an imprint of Penguin Random House, 2018.

INTERNET SITES

Historic Royal Palaces: Tower of London
http://www.hrp.org.uk/TowerOfLondon

History Channel: 6 Famous Prisoners of the Tower of London
https://www.history.com/news/6-famous-prisoners-of-the-tower-of-london

UNESCO: Tower of London
https://whc.unesco.org/en/list/488

INDEX